Alphabeach

ALPHABET ROCKS A-Z

To order additional copies of this book, contact:
Xlibris
1-888-795-4274
www.Xlibris.com
Orders@Xlibris.com

ISBN: Softcover   978-1-7960-7962-3
        Hardcover   978-1-7960-7985-2
        EBook   978-1-7960-7961-6

Print information available on the last page

Rev. date: 12/27/2019

Alphabeach

ALPHABET ROCKS A-Z

Laura Anne Crowell (Swartz)

Welcome to Alphabeach. Maybe after seeing this book you can find your own letters on rocks! After I had taken pictures of six letters in the spring I brought them in to show my middle school students. They all encouraged me to keep looking for the rest of the alphabet and that is how Alphabeach got started. I have to thank a girl named Brooke who came up with the title! It took me until of the summer and I had found all 26 letters! Now I'm looking for numbers too! Perhaps Alphanumbers will be my next creation!

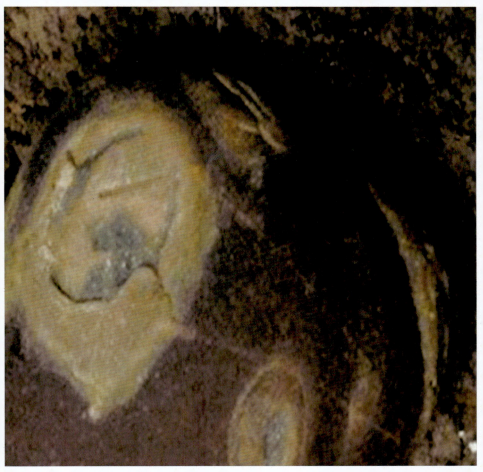

Laura Swartz is an artist and art teacher who lives near a private beach in Manomet, in Plymouth, Massachusetts. In the summer she spends time walking the beach looking for beach glass and rocks with cool designs, letters and numbers on them. She also loves to paint from photographs that she takes of the sparkling ocean, amazing clouds, and colorful sunrises and sunsets from the view of her family cottage on Sandy Neck.

Printed in the United States
By Bookmasters